THE SENSES

Seeing

CHELSEA
CLUBHOUSE

An Imprint of Chelsea House Publishers
A Haights Cross Communications Company
Philadelphia

Kimberley Jane Pryor

For Nick, Ashley and Thomas

Chelsea Clubhouse
1974 Sproul Road, Suite 400
Broomall, PA 19008-0914

The Chelsea House world wide web address is www.chelseahouse.com

Library of Congress Cataloging-in-Publication Data

Pryor, Kimberley Jane.
    Seeing / Kimberley Jane Pryor.
    p. cm. — (The senses)

    Includes index.
    Contents: Your senses — Your eyes — How you see — A message to your brain — Pupils — All kinds of sights — Seeing danger — Wearing glasses — Blindness — Protecting your eyes — Using all your senses.

    ISBN 0-7910-7555-9
    1. Vision—Juvenile literature. [1. Vision. 2. Eye. 3. Senses and sensation.] I. Title. II. Series.
    QP475.7.P79 2004
    612.8'4—dc21

                                                                    2003001174

First published in 2003 by
MACMILLAN EDUCATION AUSTRALIA PTY LTD
627 Chapel Street, South Yarra, Australia, 3141

Associated companies and representatives throughout the world.

Copyright © Kimberley Jane Pryor 2003

Page layout by Raul Diche
Illustrations by Alan Laver, Shelly Communications
Photo research by Legend Images

Printed in China

Acknowledgements
Cover photograph: children reading a book, courtesy of Corbis Digital Stock.

John Cancalosi/Auscape, p. 23; Labat-Lanceau/Auscape, p. 4; Coo-ee Picture Library, p. 27; Corbis Digital Stock, pp. 1, 9 (top and bottom left), 16 (center left); The DW Stock Picture Library, pp. 14, 28; Eyewire, p. 7; Getty Images/Image Bank, p. 29; Getty Images/Stone, p. 13; Getty Images/Taxi, pp. 5, 12, 20, 21, 24; Great Southern Stock, p. 15 (both); Dennis Sarson/Lochman Transparencies, p. 26; Nick Milton, p. 8; Photodisc, pp. 9 (top and bottom right), 16 (top left and right, center right, bottom), 17, 18; Photolibrary.com, pp. 22, 25; Photolibrary.com/SPL, p. 19; Terry Oakley/The Picture Source, p. 6.

While every care has been taken to trace and acknowledge copyright, the publisher tenders their apologies for any accidental infringement where copyright has proved untraceable. Where the attempt has been unsuccessful, the publisher welcomes information that would redress the situation.

Please note
At the time of printing, the Internet addresses appearing in this book were correct. Owing to the dynamic nature of the Internet, however, we cannot guarantee that all these addresses will remain correct.

Contents

Your Senses

You have five senses to help you learn about the world. They are sight, hearing, smell, taste, and touch.

You see the sizes, shapes, and colors of the fish with your eyes.

Seeing

You see things with your eyes. Your sense of sight helps you to figure out what an object is by its color, size, shape, movement, and distance. Sight also warns you of danger.

Your eyes tell you that this spider is dangerous.

Your Eyes

Your eyes are soft and delicate and need protection. They sit in the eye sockets, which are two hollows in the skull that surround and protect the eyes.

Your eyebrows stop sweat from trickling down your forehead into your eyes.

Eyebrows stop sweat from running into your eyes.

Your eyelids shut to stop objects and bright light from entering your eyes. They do this without you thinking about it. They also blink several times each minute, to spread tear fluid over the surface of your eyes.

Tears keep your eyes from becoming dry. When you cry, your eyes make more tears than normal.

The white part of the eye is called the **sclera**. It forms most of the eye's outer covering. The round, colored part of the eye is the **iris**. The black opening in the middle of the iris is the **pupil**.

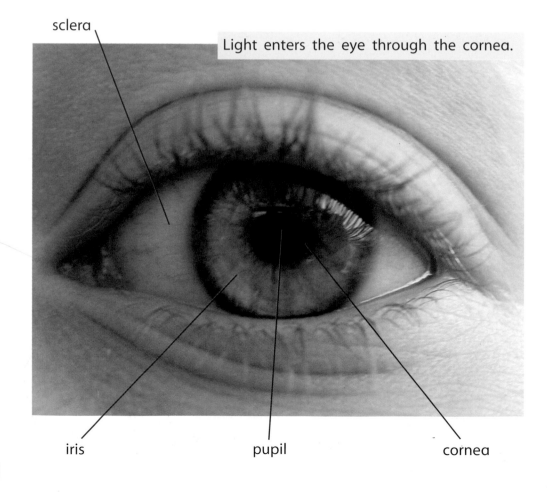

sclera

Light enters the eye through the cornea.

iris

pupil

cornea

An outer layer called the **cornea** covers both the pupil and the iris. The cornea is clear so light can pass through it and into the pupil. The pupil opens and closes to let the right amount of light into the eye.

Irises can be different colors.

How You See

When you see something, light reflects from an object and enters the eye through the cornea. The light passes through the pupil, and then through the **lens**. The lens bends the light and **focuses** it on the inner layer of the back of the eye, called the **retina**.

The image on the retina is upside down. The brain knows the object is the right way up.

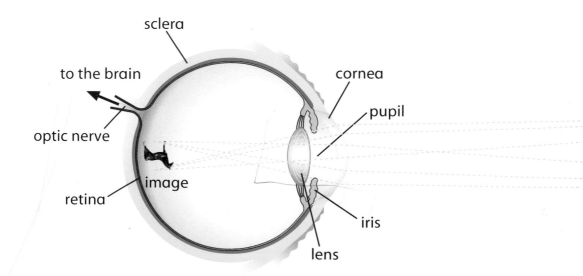

sclera

to the brain

cornea

pupil

optic nerve

image

retina

iris

lens

Cells in the retina, called rods and cones, sense the brightness and color of the light. Other cells sense movement. All these cells send signals along the **optic nerve** to the brain.

object

A Message to Your Brain

The cells in your eyes send messages to your brain. Then, your brain decides what you have seen and whether you should do something about it.

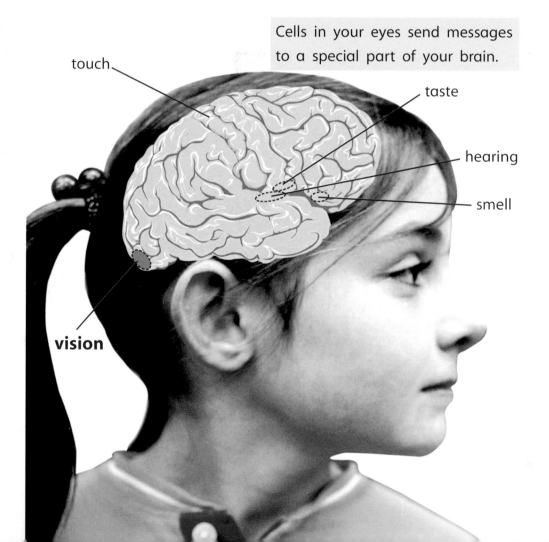

Cells in your eyes send messages to a special part of your brain.

touch

taste

hearing

smell

vision

Your eyes help you to catch a beach ball.

When someone throws a beach ball to you, your eyes send messages to your brain. Then your brain sends a message to your arms and hands to tell them to catch the beach ball.

Pupils

The iris and pupil control the amount of light that enters the eye. Muscles in the iris make the pupil smaller in bright light. This stops too much light from entering the eye and damaging the retina. The iris's muscles make the pupil bigger in dim light to let in more light so you can see better.

Pupils change size to let the right amount of light into the eyes.

Try this!

Watch your pupils change size

- ⭐ Sit in a dark room with your eyes open.
- ⭐ After 10 minutes turn the lights on and look into a mirror.
- ⭐ Watch your pupils get smaller in the bright light.

Pupils are bigger in dim light.

Pupils are smaller in bright light.

15

All Kinds of Sights

In very dim light, rods and other cells in the retinas in your eyes help you to see sizes, shapes, movement, and distance. But you cannot see colors when there is very little light. The cones in your retinas need more light to let you see colors.

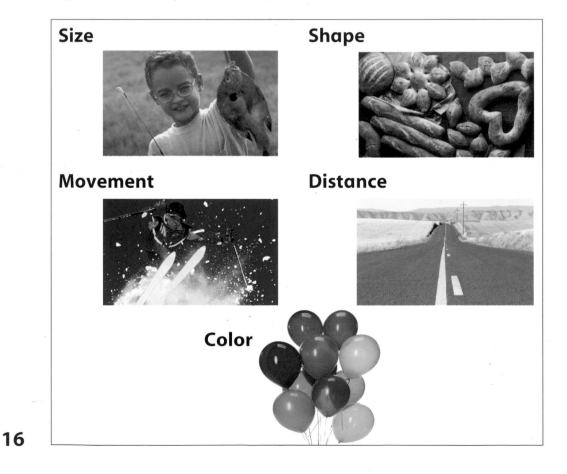

Size

Shape

Movement

Distance

Color

Try this!

Ask a parent or teacher for help.

Night shapes

⭐ Go outside on a dark night and look around you.

⭐ Look carefully at the shapes of the trees and buildings.

At night, you can tell that an object is a tree by its shape, but you will not see colors.

At night, you can see shapes but not colors.

17

Colors

Most people have three kinds of cones in their retinas. Each cone is sensitive to either red, green, or blue light. When you look at a paint palette, the cones in your retinas allow you to see the colors and they send messages to your brain.

The cones in your retinas let you see colors and fine details.

Try this!

Ask a parent or teacher for help.

Color blindness

⚙ Look at the picture of dots.

⚙ What colors can you see?

⚙ What else can you see in the picture?

People who are color blind cannot see every color. Their retinas have fewer red, green, or blue cones than normal. In this picture of dots, most people see the number 8 in the center. But people who have some color blindness may see the number 3 or no number at all.

This picture helps to test whether a person is color blind.

Size, shape, movement, and distance

When someone throws a ball to you, your eyes tell you that the ball is small, round, and moving toward you. Your brain sends a message to your arms and hands to tell them to swing the bat and hit the ball.

Your eyes help you to know how fast a ball is moving.

The lens in your eye becomes thinner when you look at distant objects.

The lens in your eye changes shape so you can see near and distant objects. When you look at things in the distance, the lens becomes thinner. When you look at nearby objects, the lens becomes thicker.

21

Seeing Danger

Your sense of sight helps warn you of danger. You use your eyes to look for cars before you cross a road. Your eyes also tell you the color of the traffic light that gives the message to stop or go.

The color of the traffic light tells you when it is safe to go.

Your eyes tell you if a person is angry or whether an animal is likely to be dangerous.

Your eyes warn you that this snake is likely to be dangerous.

Wearing Glasses

Some people wear glasses to help them see better. People who are farsighted can see objects that are far away, but they cannot see objects close to them clearly. They wear glasses to help them see nearby objects.

People who are farsighted wear glasses to help them read and write.

People who are nearsighted can see objects that are close to them, but they cannot see far away objects clearly. They wear glasses to help them see distant objects.

People who are nearsighted wear glasses to help them see things that are far away.

Blindness

People who are blind have very little or no **vision**. Some people are born without sight. Some people become blind because they have had an eye disease or an eye **injury**.

People who are blind may use guide dogs or canes when walking.

People who are blind may use white sticks known as canes or guide dogs to help them move around easily and safely. They may read books printed in **braille**, which is an alphabet of raised bumps.

People use their fingers to read braille.

Protecting Your Eyes

Your sense of sight is important and helps keep you safe. So, protect your eyes to keep them healthy!

- ⚙ Wear sunglasses when you are outside.
- ⚙ Walk when you carry sharp objects such as scissors.
- ⚙ Use good lighting when you read.
- ⚙ Do not sit too close to your computer or television.
- ⚙ Stand away from firecrackers.

Sunglasses protect your eyes from bright sunlight.

Safety goggles protect your eyes in science classes at school.

You can protect your eyes from injury by wearing safety glasses or goggles when you:

⭐ play sports such as baseball or racquetball

⭐ do science experiments at school.

Using All Your Senses

You need your senses to see, hear, smell, taste, and touch things. The best way to learn about the world is to use all your senses.

Did You Know?
Your sense of sight is your most important sense. Most of the information in your brain comes from your eyes.

Did You Know?
Each eye gives you a slightly different view of the world. This helps you to know how far away something is.

Did You Know?
Birds have excellent sight. When an eagle is flying, it can see a snake hundreds of feet below.

Glossary

braille	an alphabet of raised dots pressed into paper, which is read using the fingertips
cornea	the clear outer layer of the eye that covers the iris and pupil
focuses	makes a clear picture
injury	damage done to a part of the body
iris	the colored part of the eye; muscles in the iris control the size of the pupil.
lens	a clear part of the eye that bends light rays to focus them on the retina
optic nerve	a nerve that carries messages from cells in the retina to the brain
pupil	the opening in the iris that changes size to control the amount of light that enters the eye
retina	the inner lining of the back of the eye; the retina contains light-sensitive cells.
sclera	the white outer layer of the eye that covers all but the front of the eye
vision	the sense of sight

Index

Web Sites

You can go to these web sites to learn more about the sense of sight:

http://www.kidshealth.org/kid/body/eye_SW.html

http://howstuffworks.com/eye.htm

http://yucky.kids.discovery.com/noflash/body/pg000142.html

http://faculty.washington.edu/chudler/sight.html